My Conversational Poetical Love

Ancel Mondia

Ukiyoto Publishing

All global publishing rights are held by

Ukiyoto Publishing

Published in 2023

Content Copyright © Ancel Mondia

ISBN 9789359206578

*All rights reserved.
No part of this publication may be reproduced,
transmitted, or stored in a retrieval system, in
any form by any means, electronic, mechanical,
photocopying, recording or otherwise, without
the prior permission of the publisher.*

*The moral rights of the authors have been
asserted.*

*This is a work of fiction. Names, characters,
businesses, places, events, locales, and incidents
are either the products of the author's
imagination or used in a fictitious manner. Any
resemblance to actual persons, living or dead, or
actual events is purely coincidental.
This book is sold subject to the condition that it
shall not by way of trade or otherwise, be lent,
resold, hired out or otherwise circulated, without
the publisher's prior consent, in any form of
binding or cover other than that in which it is
published.*

Contents

Twin Flame	1
In The End	3
Valentine	4
The Distorted and The Divine	5
The Us and The Odds	6
Drunk Text	7
The Question and The Answer	8
To the bone	9
She's the one	10
Raw Emotions	11
Intrusive Thoughts	12
Mixed Signals	13
Lightbulb Moment	14
Radio Silence	15
Love Lockdown	17
White Lie	18
Third Wheel	19
Black Sheep	20
Out of the blue	21

Wild Card	22
Earth Angel	23
Divine Counterpart	25
About the Author	26

Twin Flame

Back and forth, I say yes and no
Unsure if I should love you so
Fear of pain tells me not to go
But I want you to be my beau

Do not be frightened by my light
I know you keep me in your sight
Break the silence and make it right
For this love, I will also fight

You have worked for wealth and power
But you want me as your lover
I am your home, future partner
Let us build a life together

Do you want to come to me fast
I am here to make this love last
Our distance is thing of the past
For us, the world is not too vast

Let us dive in this connection
Explore our hearts' destination
The time has come for our union
We have been each other's person

In The End

I know that you have felt the same
So don't doubt to give me your name
Heal your mind from fake love syndrome
Welcome me to light up our home
Give in to love you can't defeat
Let me take your passenger seat
Don't fight your divine counterpart
We're not fated to be apart
No matter how far you wander
You can't escape your soul lover
Though you're on the earth's other side
You know in my heart you reside
It's our love we'll choose to defend
As we'll surely meet in the end

Valentine

When can I hug my man that feels like teddy bear

Will he kiss me with the lipstick I love to wear

When can I taste his love that smells as chocolate

Will he see the sparks in my eyes so passionate

When can he treat me as his one and only rose

Will I possess the chances of having him close

When can my man take me out for a special date

Will I believe we are soulmates and trust our fate

When can we both be together and feel so fine

Will he and I meet as each other's Valentine

The Distorted and The Divine

You lived with the distorted feminine
Who acted like a mere subordinate
And she became your typical woman
She manipulated your soul and mind
By wickedly playing as the victim
Anyone who was different from her
You saw as the distorted feminine

But you knew me your divine feminine
Who was actually your only equal
You believed as your ideal woman
I liberated your spirit and heart
By genuinely living as the empress
Nobody could be similar to me
You saw me as your divine feminine

The Us and The Odds

You thought there was no one who could change you
And you prioritized money and work
You had never been so emotional
You thought there was no one who had loved you
People expected you to be the same
Because your ways had become natural
It was neither you nor they wanted change

But you said I was the one who changed you
As you valued relationship and love
And you had become so emotional
You said I was the one who had loved you
People attempted to make you the same
But your ways became new and different
Together you and I became the change

Drunk Text

The taste of alcohol wetted my mouth
It heated my body and drowned my mind
I pulled out my phone and typed a message
Was about to send but I deleted
I bottled up my feelings when sober
Was shy and intimidated by you
Stared at the screen and read our past convo
You did friendzone me and I did ghost you
But our ending did not sit well with me
Was not over you so I gained courage
Wanted to know you more than alcohol
You disturbed my spirit and owned my heart
I typed a message and sent it to you
But to my drunk text you did not reply

The Question and The Answer

You asked me why would I opt to love you
When you gave me none to reciprocate
For it was never you who received first
So you chose to do what you thought was right
And not the love you had ever wanted
But you had known you could not escape love
So you tried to return to me your life

I told you I just opted to love you
As I gave you my all for you to take
It did not matter if I received last
So I chose to do what I had wanted
And not the thing that others thought was right
And I had known I could not reject love
So I accepted you back in my life

To the bone

When your small eyes shone
My whole mind was blown
Your bright smile had grown
And I just felt thrown
From your so sweet tone
Delight I had known
Your warm hands alone
Were my comfort zone
My all was your own
When your light had flown
My sole heart of stone
Loved you to the bone

She's the one

Though she styles or dyes her hair
And she has changeable air
Still he cannot help but stare
Sometimes she's tanned, sometimes fair
Lips can be colored or bare
She alone remains his pair
Different clothes she will wear
For she has mood swings to bear
He thinks she's beyond compare
She's not anywhere, she's rare
She gives glare but she takes care
He adores her, he can swear
Though she can cause smile and tear
In spite of her past affair
She's the one he'll never share

Raw Emotions

I've experienced raw emotions for you
They're strong and natural, what can I do
Now may I ask you, do you feel them too
I wish they're for me, not for someone new
Nor for someone in the past that you knew
But where am I with my feelings so true
Do you know or will you see my value
I have no idea, I have no clue
The clear answer may come out of the blue
Now I'm fine seeing you as distant view
Patience with little hope is my virtue
Maybe we shall meet in a shared venue
And the days that come before that are few
Now let me process my feelings that brew
So that my lips I won't anxiously chew
With prayer that your love will see me through

Intrusive Thoughts

You are my intrusive thoughts, don't you know
Disturbing memories of you just flow
Your presence and absence make me feel low
I can't control notions of you that grow
You stay in my mind for days in a row
In every dream, you repeatedly show
It is you that make my spinning world slow
I am getting anxious to see you glow
But it is your time I wish to borrow
It is you that can fill in the hollow
You may not see but I have love below
Hope I am your significant fellow
For you are the soul I want to follow
Allow me to think and admire you so
Until we both say yes, and never no
Now end my intrusive thoughts with hello

Mixed Signals

You keep sending me mixed signals, why dear
You turn hot and cold, is it due to fear
Have not you let anybody come near
Stop being inconsistent and be clear
Be true to me, is it too hard to hear
I have been waiting for you for a year
Don't you appear only to disappear
I'll give this chance for you to be sincere
You can never solve us by drinking beer
Nor by running away just like a deer
I'll understand if you love your career
I won't take away what gives you the cheer
Believe me, I will never interfere
So stop making things between us unclear
Tell me if you're just being insincere
So I'll move on or I'll wait for you here

Lightbulb Moment

I pray that you'll have a lightbulb moment
So you'll understand why we turned silent
I hope we'll start anew in the present
By having the better and right judgment
Let's put an end to prideful cold treatment
I think that I am done being patient
Remember, you're no longer a student
And I can already pay my payment
Each of us can become a good parent
We've grown wise, we're no longer innocent
But our love has never turned different
So tell me when will you do the movement
And I will process every document
Let's submit and act on same commitment
With you, I'll always be in fulfillment
This epiphany is your contentment

Radio Silence

There is radio silence between you and me

It is your absence that I always feel and see

I expect a sign from you that will give me glee

But our distance makes me ask should I set you free

You are never mine, should I believe and agree

But why did you make me happy to some degree

Was there something from me you wished to guarantee

Did I fail you so you just pulled back completely

Have you thought we can be missed opportunity

We can be an unfinished business, don't you flee

If I need a closure, tell me the real story

If we should reconcile, give me apology

Is the present separation temporary

Or is it here and now, all should end totally

Please give me the answer when you become ready

Break the radio silence so I'll hear clearly

Love Lockdown

I'm in love lockdown, can you ever tell
I have been hiding mixed feelings that dwell
How did it happen, I just know I fell
You made me believe in heaven and hell
My cash can't buy your love that you don't sell
And it irritates me like dirt to shell
Against my only love I can't rebel
You're always on my mind, is this your spell
My deep fantasies of you hurt and swell
I think I need to confess to get well
But I get afraid that you shall just yell
You do nothing but it seems you compel
I want to submit but I feel unwell
But my secrets I desire to dispel
Many adore you so, can I excel
I fear we'll end here and you bid farewell

White Lie

I am sorry for telling a white lie
I'm protecting us from the evil eye
You know we have an unbreakable tie
Now please have relief and let out a sigh
You must not doubt, I shall not make you cry
I value you with a respect so high
Have faith in me, you do not need to spy
Tell me your worries, don't just bid goodbye
I am sure I love you, do not ask why
I shall be with you through days wet and dry
Please believe me, I have no other guy
My love is too precious for them to buy
You are the rightful owner till we die
It's only your both hands I'll take to fly
I am proud of you, there's no need to vie
You are mine alone, others must not pry

Third Wheel

I really don't want to be the third wheel
For I need the love of my own to feel
It's you, my man, that circumstances steal
A sign tells me that you still need to heal
I'm not the third party, I'm the real deal
You will know and see as time will reveal
Be prepared, you will no longer conceal
The truth that to you, others don't appeal
I really do care if you want me still
And if ever before me, you will kneel
I will get over my thoughts that are ill
So we both can make our love last with zeal
My man, it is only time we can kill
Our love for each other will remain real
Take me away from lovers quite unreal
And let's breathe life to our dream as we will

Black Sheep

I have been considered as the black sheep
But I have changed when I know someone deep
It's you that wake me up from the long sleep
I've begun to prize you for you're not cheap
I have worked hard so your love I can keep
Please do accept me and don't make me weep
For in my subconscious, you always creep
The truth that I want you, I just can't sweep
So I've improved myself, I've made a leap
I wish to come close so I just don't peep
You are the true love I desire to reap
For you save me from life that looks like heap
Through my whole being, your kind real words seep
My statement about you is true, not steep
So allow me to fetch you with a beep
Together let's travel life through our jeep

Out of the blue

You have come in my life out of the blue
You have won my heart without any clue
My world has begun to have a new hue
Since my spirit has known the love from you
Please let me to provide you with love too
I shall sustain your good fate as your due
I know we deserve us, I really do
I don't want anybody else to woo
I love you, the words I hope you shall coo
When we both commit, blessings shall ensue
So it's my love offer, you must not shoo
I've fallen by surprise and without cue
But I'm certain what shall last is us two
You're the story I don't wish to undo
So accept my love that is pure and true
With loving you, I shall never be through

Wild Card

Was it spur-of-the-moment when I said I fell hard

You had the influence and qualities of wild card

You seemed to take over my heart that I used to guard

I honestly would not mind the past that made you scarred

I would even help you heal from happenings that marred

Your happiness and freedom I would not disregard

I would make sure that my love would not make you feel barred

For your absence was the rejection that deeply jarred

So please come back to me in my life where you once starred

And let's start anew as I would give you my regard

Earth Angel

I'm not an earth angel, stop feeding your delusion

I'm just an average human, far from perfection

I'm maybe the being from your manifestation

But I am a complex and difficult creation

Explore my world before you give me admiration

My existence you must comprehend with precision

I don't welcome spirits that only bring destruction

I'm my own life, don't treat me just an inspiration

You must have your own identity and ambition

And in your space, I can only be an addition

Your support and encouragement towards completion

As we both, you and I, are in reciprocation

I'm not an earth angel, but I'll be your companion

Divine Counterpart

After I learned to connect to myself with love
I met you, my divine counterpart, from above
After I completed myself and became whole
I was able to deeply connect with your soul
You supported my energy by being you
Sharing our authentic worlds was easy to do
Together, we continued to reflect and grow
The community witnessed the light we did show
We ended imbalance and turned integrated
From ego, it was ourselves we liberated
Our need for power was replaced by compassion
As we embraced the truth of our imperfection
We both savored the process of discovery
As our partnership stayed in bliss and harmony

About the Author

Ancel Mondia

Ancel Mondia was awarded Fiction - Woman Writer of the Year by Ukiyoto Publishing in 2023.

www.ingramcontent.com/pod-product-compliance
Lightning Source LLC
LaVergne TN
LVHW041601070526
838199LV00046B/2091